Cultivating Faith: Gardening as an Experiential Bible Study

Teryl Cartwright

DEDICATION

To the Glory of God

CONTENTS

1   One Cent Seeds   1

2   Mud Pies   9

3   Tree Surgeon   17

4   Stolen Away   25

5   George Washington's   31
     Axe

6   God Plays with Food   37

7   Perennial Parables   44

8   Paul Planted and Apollos   53
     Watered

9   Finding a Place to Grow   59

10   Hope: Buried Treasure   66

11   Biblical Garden   72
     Adventure

12   Wheat Fields   78

     Bibliography   84

     About the Author   86

Acknowledgements

Thank you to the inaugural class of this study!

It was ironic to have a gardening class online
but I am grateful to Eddie, Tammy, Jim, Holly,
Linda, Shannon, Sheryl, Janet, Andrew,
and Patricia.

I am honored to offer this at the Institute for
Discipleship. You are all very special people
and I am blessed to have met you for this
faith cultivation.

Thanks also to the Center for Spiritual Formation
who offered me a chance to do this as a webinar.

One Cent Seeds

Before you read what I have written, set a timer for three minutes and using a pen, fill these lined pages without stopping until the timer rings. Let this Freewriting[1] exercise give you a chance to clear your mind, see what you are thinking, capture the to-do list or expectations you have, record the things you don't want to forget, or save the prayer you need to offer. Even if you don't know what to write, write that too. Just connect the thoughts to pen to paper. I'll see you on the other side.

_____

_____

_____

_____

_____

_____

_____

_____

_____

_____

_____

When I was a little girl, a great joy of winter was receiving the seed catalog to pore over and dream of what to grow. One catalog had a one-cent seed packet for children that had a mix of vegetable and flower seeds. I was about six when my parents let me pay a penny, and I planted my garden so I could be like Pop and Dad. They had fantastic gardens, and I wanted mine to be like theirs. I saw the beauty in the harvest and the ideal in the work.

I realize now the seed packet I received was the mixture of leftover seeds culled and cleaned out from the nursery's seed packaging machines. These seeds were mostly unidentifiable, and the larger ones like the beans and treated corn seeds were scant. Some were even broken and cut. It wasn't the garden of my dreams, but to start, to be given seeds as a child was a precious gift. In the hands of a slightly disappointed but still optimistic child, those seeds were given a second chance. They were seeds, and they were mine. The only ones I think that made it that year with my amateur hands were the marigolds. Still, those leftover seeds all grew. They grew that part inside of me that loved gardens and wanted more. Even seeds that don't seem to have a harvest can do so in other ways.

Each year after that, I remember the excitement in my home to get those seed catalogs right after Christmas. Did you get them too? It gave hope to the winter months, and imagination stirred for the joy and possibilities in the year ahead. The pictures and the descriptions just inspired me to dream about being a gardener, content, and productive. Now I use the internet and see "what's new" and feel those same stirrings to cultivate a garden again. I still dream and smile. And these thoughts of gardening today reawaken my memories even more.

I remember Pop's garden was at the top of a hill that was really steep to climb but somehow it was fitting to plant closer to God. Grandma Smith's meticulously kept garden was smaller and across the flat yard while her flower beds along the outside of her home were inviting and close by. My aunt's vegetable garden was hidden in the back of her house near the woods, but the roses out front and the morning glories were what drew your eyes. My mom's indoor aloe and spider plant were just as beloved as the lilac and lobelia outdoors. And while Dad had the apple tree, rhubarb, and asparagus, and Pop was known for his tomatoes, there was room for other plants to be part of my childhood memories. The gardens all had a style. Each gardener showed a different reason for planting and cultivating. They all taught me something, and yet it's only in going back that I can recognize what I didn't know then.

What gardens do you remember growing up? Where they the marigolds you grew in class to take home for Mother's Day or the courageous plants that went through your experiments for the science fair? Were they the bulbs you planted that you got from your neighbor or even the plants you grew in the aquarium for all the fish?

I invite you to take some time to tell others about your gardens, from the potted plants to the fields of a farm. I know the conversation will be different if you are a casual gardener who has a "Christmas cactus" that blooms at Thanksgiving versus a commercial gardener that talks of yield per acre, but we all have our stories that need to be shared. Please tell your stories too.

Whether it was a Jacob's tears plant I bought or the pink poinsettia an anonymous friend gave me at Christmas that I have managed to somehow keep alive, there are secret gardens of all sizes that have meaning, that we give meaning in our life. Till the soil of your memories and my prayer is that you will unearth more.

Take a break now and talk about gardens with someone. Don't plow ahead to get to the end of the chapter. Give yourself space to look back and see what was grown in your life. What did you notice? What does it mean to you now?

In order to cultivate faith, we need to look to the Bible. It all begins for us in a garden. We are tending the Lord's garden, and all that means. And then we come to the forbidden fruit tree. What is it about knowledge that we just have to get it?

Why is the trust and love of God often not enough for us?

It all started out well. Do you notice that Eve saw that the fruit was good, pleasing to the eye[2]? The ability to appreciate, to see beauty, and perceive goodness, is a God-given gift. Yet, we can see the temptation here. It is the dark side of appreciation, the wanting of something that belongs to others for ourselves.

I believe coveting, our tripping over the tenth commandment, is why we have trouble keeping the other nine. There is something we covet in each commandment that we try to take from others. Even before God gave the Ten Commandments, we mourn that Adam and Eve broke several in one act. In consuming what they shouldn't, they were consumed by their greed. We are too.

We think of Eve and then Adam's fear of missing out and taking what they covet. We can see it in King Ahab's lust, stealing Naboth's vineyard[3]. We can see it in the parable Jesus told of the tenants killing the owner's son to take possession of the vineyard[4].

As we go back over the gardens of others we have appreciated, we need to be aware of what we covet. Gardens often have fences to keep out predators, and with God's help, we need to drive out the foxes, the snakes, and sometimes ourselves.

I know you may fret about getting to the end of this chapter, but as a spiritual practice, take a prayer walk now for at least ten minutes. Put this book down and see in your prayer walk. It can be a virtual walk or, weather permitting, a physical one. See the gardens around you. They might be fruit, vegetable, flower, lawn, or landscape. Visualize and pray for those gardens of your neighbors. If they are admirable and pleasing to the eye, praise God because it is not only the gardener's effort that brings forth the best. If the gardens are not growing well, pray for their healing and restoration because a garden is not necessarily a reflection of the gardener but could be struggling through pests and conditions you cannot see.

We've walked and talked about past and present gardens that we've seen to begin to prepare for the future. While it is helpful to use gardens as analogies and experiential learning to cultivate faith, we know that we rely on God as our Gardener. So let us start with a prayer to water the ground and soften the soil to grow.

> *Gracious God, how incredible are your gardens! In the colors and structures, we see Eden's memories, and we anticipate the Revelation of heaven's garden to come. We cannot know what all you are growing in our season, but we ask that you plant us closer to you. Give us your love to shelter us and let us abide in you to be fruitful. Hear the words and prayers of each reader too. May your Holy Spirit be with us so that as two or three are gathered even in a written sharing of thoughts, you transcend our boundaries and limitations of time and imagination to be with us in both places to help us grow together. In Jesus' name, may thy will be done and your kingdom garden come. Amen.*

Think of what you could plant and the stories you could share from the Bible as part of this cultivation! I am offering you some Bible passages for you to fashion into a Bible study. Like seeds, we can plant them in many ways. I am giving you my "two-cents worth" seeds packet, the widow's mite, for you to decide how to use and what to learn. If you are wondering what you can do with them, the least I would offer is to see them as a devotional and reflect on whether they grow together. You have room to take notes here, but don't pass up a chance to pray about how they can enrich your faith. Let's discover what's new to glean from them.

Genesis 3

Hosea 10:12

Romans 8:28

2 Corinthians 9:10

Mud Pies

Prayer: *Lord, may I offer you the firstfruits of my gardening and the firstfruits of my heart. May my best thoughts be given to you, and my worst confessed. Gracious God, grow your Spirit within me and bury my sins in the dust. I am but a creation from the earth, but you have breathed in me life, and I am yours. Please help me garden so that others see you in my work, my produce, my character, and my humility. To you be the glory, Amen.*

Your Prayer:

Again, I bring up a memory from childhood, which happened when I was around six or seven. I lived in a house where we had someone else's cornfield beside us and a great field of horses across a road I wasn't allowed to cross. My brother and I were allowed to roam the woods on the other side of the house, and we played with no other children around, for our sister wasn't born yet. We often amused ourselves in unusual ways.

In this time, my mom had given us aluminum pie pans to fill up with mud and pretend to bake in the summer sun. It was deep brown, chocolate-looking goo. As we played outside, I found seeds from various weeds and made a pattern on top of the mud pie with Queen Anne's lace decorating the center. We then asked about selling the mud pie, and my parents, with a great sense of humor, allowed my brother and me to set up a sign along the road and wait. One man actually stopped for a mud pie, but when he saw what it was, he shook his head and drove away. I was disappointed he didn't buy it. It took me a few years to understand that others had a different idea of what a mud pie was and why it was so funny to sell real ones even with the pretty patterns on top.

Cain must have been upset about his rejected offering too. Like his dad, he was a gardener, and yet his best (or perhaps not his best, as some commentators speculate) didn't please God. He had a choice as to what to do about it, but he decided to take out the competition rather than fix his own garden and gardening[5].

We started with Adam tending God's garden, and then he is cursed to make a living from it while fully relying on God to provide the growth of the seed, the water for the plants, and the right weather for it to produce[6]. We labor to produce that which was easy for God to create. The eating of the fruit from the tree of knowledge taught that we desire to be like God, but in eating the fruit that we've grown afterward, leaving the Garden of Eden, we learn we are not God. Our best efforts are nothing without him, and our gardens can also grow without us.

Do you have mud pies in your life? Even if today, if someone could package and sell a pretty pattern seed starter kit as a profitable mud pie, where are the weed seeds and mud we dress up to look like something more than it really is?

What are you going to grow in your garden? That's a question that tells us a lot about ourselves. Fill up an aluminum pie pan with some mud and plant something.

I've seen the bean seeds you can buy that have the imprinted message "I love you" on them that appears only after they sprout. What messages do you think that you are giving (intentionally or not) in your gardening choices?

What messages do you think God is sharing in your gardening results?

Before you plan your garden, have you found out about gardening purposes? While some do garden for a living, there are all kinds of gardens to consider. For instance, the English country garden seeks to be in harmony with nature while the French formal garden seeks to master nature[7]. When God gave his command, was it to steward or subdue the earth? How do we do it? Are the forms of gardening something we can look at for our soul gardens? Are we mastering nature or our own natures? Are we seeking harmony with God's creation or God himself?

Think about how you garden. Do you look to fit into the land or to change it? What does this mean to us spiritually?

When you have moved into a new home, do you keep the trees and flowers, or do you take them out and put in your own? What does this question have to do with our practices in our ministries and churches?

Take a few minutes to find out the rules or ideals of different gardens. While I have mentioned the English and French gardens, there are garden forms from China and Spain and the Mediterranean, to name a few more. Some styles favor symmetry, and some use the land the way it is to bring the best from it. Some develop gardens like art or architecture, while others work with gardens as a science or industry. What did you find that was of interest to you?

What did you discover that is helpful for you to connect to your faith and spiritual development?

Take an inventory now of your current gardens. Remember that you may have several. Your lawn can be seen as a one seed garden and your indoor plants as a year-round one. You may have seasonal gardens that you plant at different times for different reasons. As you make your lists, why do you have these gardens? What are their purposes, or are they without one? Does it matter?

Isn't it amazing that Jesus put mud in someone's eyes to see[8]? Collect some soil and water it in a container. Let your hands get dirty. Feel the mud. I'm not asking you to put it on your eyes but to look at it, see the mud, and through it.

Pray about what God needs you to see in your life. Pray for those who are spiritually blind and include yourself in this prayer. We don't know what we aren't seeing because we don't see it without God's intervention. As a spiritual practice, think about what you need in that soil to help seeds grow. Where does that connect with you in your faith? Where DOESN'T it?

This time for the Bible verses I offer you, I'd like you to read and garden with them. Treat them like a French formal garden and create a structure to teach or share them. Consider them like a cottage garden that looks like a "vegetable garden overtaken by flowers"[9] and find the beauty in composition along with the practical "food for thought" mixed together. Go back to some of the things you found interesting in your research of gardens and your stories of gardening to see where these perspectives can complement the scriptures below.

Genesis 4

Leviticus 27:30

Deuteronomy 28:1-14

Proverbs 12:11

Isaiah 40:12; 61:11

Mark 4:26-29

Faith has often been compared to a journey, but we can also be stuck in the mud like faithful Jeremiah in the cistern[10]. When I took a look at the Bible verses that included the word "mud," most were negative. Yet gardens need mud. They need water and soil. So when we are told to "be still and know that I am God, "[11] it could mean a chance to stop and plant seeds or to rest and let God's seeds grow. As Rev. Rebecca Collison, author of Preparing the Field for Seasons, shares, we need to know what season we are in. Winters and fallow times are needed for the snow to blanket our resting land. While she focuses on the process for rural churches to thrive in each season using gardening analogies and stories[12], I plan to focus on the smaller gardens of individuals and small groups within a church.

Finally, as a closing to this chapter on mud pies and firstfruits, please do that prayer walk around and in your church. Look for the gardens, even the pictures of gardens. Are there resting places? What kinds of plants do you have – dogwood, bleeding hearts, hedges?

What do these choices and structures have to say? What are the messages that are intended? What might be the unintended ones? Are your church gardens places to visit and use, or are they for another purpose?

Now that you have all this go back and look again at your seed list. What are you going to grow this year, and why? How will your garden help grow your faith? What do you need to ask God? You can also use the space to draw it out if this helps.

Tree Surgeon

When I was in fifth grade, I wanted to be a botanist and literally save trees by grafting back on broken branches and healing them. My aunt bought me some books, one I remember on botany, a little paperback guidebook with a blue cover and one on the language of flowers, a beige hardcover, telling me what the flowers symbolize. I don't remember the third, but I still have the other two, my love of all plants still stirred by looking at them.

My own attempts at grafting as a child didn't go well. I didn't know you were supposed to pay attention to trees and branch sizes. I didn't know about covering the graft, so it didn't dry out, and so the ants didn't get at it. I didn't know there were angles to the cut and even wedges you can make to have the grafts hold better.[13]

But now there are "multi-bud" or "combination fruit trees" I can buy, though the "fruit cocktail" ones seem prevalent mostly in Australia. Some come with four or five-in-one combinations, such as varieties of apple trees. Some are even combinations of pitted fruits that include peach, apricot, cherries, and plums in one tree. Some have twenty-seven fruit, but I have yet to find one that grows nine fruit to have a grafted tree is quite Biblical. I tried to buy a grafted fruit tree in January, but they were already sold out. Interestingly, many people want them even if with help we might make some ourselves.

I am still preparing for my grafted fruit tree, even if I must wait another year. One of the interesting facts I learned in preparing for this is that you must prune the more productive branches to allow room, so the slower growers are not choked out.[14] I'm not sure if I should examine this personally as the fruit of the Spirit discipline or corporately as a church's spiritual assessment.

What do you think? Are there strengths in your growing faith that crowd out your attention to your brokenness or weak parts?

I know that I can be so wrapped up in my delight in teaching and connecting with scriptures that I don't focus as much on prayer or serving. My pride in sharing my gifts of creative ministry often needs to be pruned back. Using social media to "humble brag" can get my heart leaning toward the attention of people instead of reaching toward God.

When you think of pruning, it can be a necessary process in churches. Budgets and staffing might immediately come to mind, but I'd ask for you to frame it in a gardening context. When would you prune back successful ministries to give the struggling ones a chance? How?

What might that pruning look like in time, resources, or with the people involved?

Would it produce more faith-building to ask successful ministries to tithe their success and prune themselves for the lifting up of the more lowly?

If we are to talk gardens, then we are used to the idea of thinning seedlings in contrast to pruning for more fruitfulness. In this instance, we weed out the plants we planted and now don't want to allow room and resources for the ones that are left. I've known some gardens where the thinning is done carefully to favor the strongest and quickest growth. Yet I've also seen thinning that is random, each plant equally vibrant and filled with potential. One is plucked, and the other is given its chance more by luck than its own growing efforts.

Where do you see the church enacting any thinning practices based on current results?

Where in your personal life are you thinning out things to provide room and resources for your spiritual development?

As I shared earlier, I had wanted to be a botanist. I had studied to know trees and had this one particular oak that I saw as the ideal. I wondered if you had any ideal as far as the shape of a tree. We could talk about bonsai gardening and the fantastic shapes of trees that look like animals. Do we even examine the shape and health of our faith the same way using any preconceived ideal?

Often, people are asked to list events in their faith journey, but I thought it would be interesting to draw your faith tree. What does it ideally look like? What branches are broken that need healed? Draw it here. There are so many ways to do this, so try a few ideas and see what your faith tree looks like.

I love the saying that people can't see the forest for the trees. Sometimes the reverse is also true. We can't see the individuals when we focus on the whole. How wonderful that in one of Jesus' miracles, the partially healed man called the people "trees walking around."[15] It's an apt description, but I wonder about our own partial blindness. How can we see what we don't know we should? I wear glasses, so I have some ideas of what I should see, even if I don't wear my spiritual ones enough in my walk through the gardens with God.

For example, when we look at Jesus as the Master Gardener, we relate to Mary, who saw the resurrected Jesus but didn't see him. She was right in thinking Jesus the gardener, walking again with us in a garden, but she couldn't hold onto him there.[16] At least one thing about us being trees that move is that our fruitfulness is not limited to one place or season or kind.

Are we to prune back in some aspects or habits in ourselves as a spiritual practice, or do we pray to God for this? What is the difference?

What is the difference between the cutting down of unproductive branches and the pruning of productive branches to be more fruitful? They are both painful. How do we know which one God is doing?

I've plucked out some different Bible passages for you to read and list your insights. Graft together some ideas and questions. If it helps, picture the sentences like branches and see how they might fit together as a tree for you.

Romans 11:17-24

John 15:1-12

Isaiah 18:5, 60:21

Galatians 5:22-23

Revelation 22:1-2

Luke 6:43-45

Now that we've done some symbolic pruning and grafting, look at how you will do this as an experience. Watch some videos or read about some of the methods for both pruning and grafting. Pay attention to what you need and why you need them. Look around your yard and garden for the plants you might use.

What are some reflections you have from doing this kind of experiential gardening?

What are the next steps? What do you need to learn or do?

Compare this to your ministry. Where are you going to prune and/or graft?

When the Bible uses this to refer to people, what is the loving way this can apply to our church family and our relationships that we want to grow to be more productive and fruitful?

As we finish a brief exploration of pruning and grafting, I'm going to invite you to pretend you are a fifth-grader, someone ten-years-old. Maybe you know someone that can help you with this.

I want you to take a prayer walk. Be very open and aware of the Holy Spirit and your surroundings. You will know from this chapter and some of the previous ones what you might talk with God about on this journey. If you want to walk around your yard or neighborhood, that would be fine. If you want to walk in the woods or park or further afield, this is great too. Please take your pruning and grafting supplies with you.

I have always wondered about the road not taken[17] and path leading to path that sometimes (I have written elsewhere) does bring you back to the same place again.

Would you take the time to fix a broken branch that will not in any way profit you with fruit you will see? Would you become for me that compassionate and observant child botanist that was going to heal those trees and plants? I'm asking you to do it just because they need help from someone who knows now how to fix them. Would you take a moment and listen to the language of flowers and what it means that God caused them to bloom at this time and place for you?

I'll join you on that walk in some way. It's my prayer that we'll bear fruit that goes beyond our own garden today. Let me know what happens; you can use this space below as a journal to not forget our childhood dreams of changing the world by serving those who cannot speak.

Stolen Away

When I was in high school, our biology teacher came back from Sabbatical halfway through the school year. She started by showing off some of her prized possessions in her old display cabinet, including huge pine cones from the west coast. These items were carefully passed around the room but not too carefully. Someone dropped one of the cones, and students scrambled to collect all the seeds that popped out from the dry old thing.

The teacher was hysterical, frantically grabbing the seeds. She implied she shouldn't have the pine cones and made it clear we definitely shouldn't have any of those seeds. Most of the seeds were on the floor, but one flew up and landed on my desk beside my books, hidden from her view. I don't know why I didn't give it back. I had helped pick up the other seeds from under our feet. But not that one seed. Instead, I hid it and took it home.

At first, I didn't dare plant it for fear I'd get in trouble. Then I didn't plant it because I didn't want to mess it up. I knew it had only one chance to grow. For years it sat in my jewelry box, a treasure with potential. A seed of a gigantic tree -- I could only dream of seeing it grow someday.

I thought about planting it in a park, and years later, people wondering how it got there. I considered planting it in our yard, but I didn't want to be found out. In college, I took a science class that involved germinating seeds. I learned a few methods, but still, I waited years and years.

I took the seed out more than thirty years later, soaked it overnight, tried wrapping it in a paper towel, and put it in a plastic bag for ten days. It didn't grow. It was too late. I was too late. Maybe that failure was appropriate for an ill-gotten gain. Yet, it wasn't the seed's fault. It would have never had the chance in the display

25

cabinet. Yet this doesn't excuse that it was a stolen seed from a teacher who stole it from a park. What would you risk to have and grow a seed?

Have you ever taken a seed that didn't belong to you to grow?

What do you hold onto that is a symbol of a failure in character?

What do you do with a "bad seed"?

Now, as I am writing this book, I have another story about seeds. I found some seeds growing in my informal compost, the slimy gunk of old food sprouting unexpectedly. I felt this must mean something because I am writing a book about cultivating faith, and I was given a surprise garden.

What could I do? I rescued two seedlings that would die otherwise, and I planted them in a flower pot put above my kitchen sink. One died. The transplant was too much for it. The other is growing, but something even stranger happened. Another sprout grew as tall as the survivor beside it a few days later. Yet, I don't know where that seed came from because the small bit of decomposing vegetable waste that came with the first didn't have any growth that I could see. I don't even know what plants they are yet since they only have their "seed leaves" or cotyledons.

You can have bad seeds kept in jewelry boxes and good seeds growing in the garbage. I am thinking a lot about that and why God would have this happen. What would you share about this?

I viewed videos about growing seeds, and maybe you'll find time to do it too. I watched a man who wanted to see which lemon tree seeds grew best.[18] He put some in a damp paper towel and plastic bag and put them in a closet for two weeks. Another set of seeds he peeled the hard outer shell away and planted in the soil. Another set he just planted as they were in the soil. Can you guess which grew best for him?

The set of seeds planted in soil without extra measures won the germination rate. For all those who will claim other methods are better, this is just what he shared. He posted videos of the growth of those lemons over the next year. The regular seed lemons grew differently because of their genetics, for they were in the same place and treated the same with watering and sun and soil. Yet, they were the ones that flourished.

I'm sharing this talk of seeds to get to other things we link to seeds. Ideas, fresh starts, money, investors are just a few. What new things are you storing in a jewelry box, waiting for the "right time" or "right place" for them to be planted?

Why? What would you need to grow that new thing?

What new things are you seeing grow in the unexpected spot, ignoring them because of their inconvenient timing or their undesired location?

Why? What assumptions or desires do you have that keep you rooted in refusing to grow?

What connects to your faith in these two answers?

What are your stories of plants persisting to grow and those who broke your heart for not trying?

I've seen plants jump flower pots, and a heart-shaped leaf grow from the crack of a curb, the rockiest of ground. I've watched crops I planted with care and hope that never make it past their seed leaves in the tenderest, tilled soil.

In the first chapter, we talked of seeds and why we grow them. This chapter looks at what grows from seeds and why. Please read and write your reflection about the following verses:

Job 14:7

Matthew 7:17

Proverbs 13:12

Psalm 1:1-3

This time I want you to start looking at the Bible for verses about seeds and planting. You will encounter some of them later in the book in different contexts, but for now, put down some new things here, Bible verses you have chosen to grow along with mine.

What verses did you choose, what did you want to share, and why did you choose them?

Scripture 1:

Scripture 2:

Scripture 3:

Scripture 4:

Of course, experiential gardening includes actual hands-on cultivation. Choose some seeds and pick a method to germinate them. Mark your calendar for when they grow and keep a growing journal for at least ten days after they start to develop. What spiritual practices can you start the same time you plant the seeds?

How does it help to have a visual reminder of something growing as you put this new thing into practice?

What are some ways it does not help you with your faith?

I want you to consider the ideas of "good seeds" and "bad seeds again." How do we know which is which?

Why do you think God made "seed leaves" that make many beginning sprouts look so much alike that they are hard to distinguish from each other?

When has some new spiritual growth been hard for you to identify in your life? Who has helped you figure out where you are growing best in your faith? Who has challenged you to grow in a place or time that was difficult for your faith?

As you can see, the seed analogy can be useful to look at our personal lives and our lives together in the church. We can give young children plants to care for when we teach about faith development. We can celebrate plants that thrive and mourn those who don't while sharing stories of growing from the Bible. I hope that you won't stop growing from here!

George Washington's Axe

Like the thirty-year-old seed, I had another time in which I delayed my gardening. This, though, was for an opposite reason. I planted two Nanking cherry trees in my yard. They were large and mature enough to produce fruit within a few years. They didn't. One didn't even make it past the second year.

I reenacted the parable of the unfruitful fig tree[19]. I gave the one that survived three years, then four, then five before I cut it down. It had grown crooked at a forty-five-degree angle, unwilling to be straightened. I had been so excited when it bloomed the first year, but it never produced fruit the second when I expected it.

I learned that you grieve over plants that never lived up to their potential. It's easy to regret such an investment of time and resources. I hate to give up on anything, but I needed this lesson as much as the tree.

What stories do you have of the plants you have had to cut down or give up?

Is there a pattern for you as to how long you will try or what you do to try to get something to grow?

What lessons from this kind of gardening do you apply to your own ministries?

Take this time now to pray. Do you pray for the losses or for God to prevent them now?

You gardeners know what I, in hindsight, didn't. I hadn't realized that the cherry tree wasn't self-fertilizing. When it was the lone fruit tree, it couldn't produce any fruit. I had let the tree down. I hadn't replaced the one that died, so the crooked one had a good reason for being unfruitful that all the fertilizer and watering couldn't fix.

What connection does this one unfruitful tree have for our spiritual fruit production?

Where do you need to make sure you aren't trying to be fruitful for God without help or companionship?

Of course, you can read about Jesus cursing the fig tree that gave the appearance of fruitfulness but wasn't. In either passage you chose, you'll see the mention of Jerusalem and understand the connection. Yet how does the fig tree connect to your life, your city, your fruitfulness?

What are the signs of bearing fruit that are true and not a façade?

One of the interesting things I discovered in taking this gardening analogy to heart was discovering the need for some fruit trees to have "chill hours."[20] In my research, I found some fruit trees need to have a minimum set of time in winter to bear fruit in season. They rest during this time at a certain temperature, usually between freezing and forty-five degrees Fahrenheit. Without the right range of chill hours, trees can come out of dormancy too soon or too late, not blooming in time. While extreme cold can kill them, they actually flourish in the spring and summer if they have gone through this colder season where they are forced to wait.

I'm not sure what season you are in to be reading this right now. For you, what is your season of fruitfulness?

Is it possible to be in different seasons for different parts of faith? Why or why not?

What if your church is in a different season of fruitfulness than you?

How do you know what spiritual season a group or family might be in?

Some gardeners that have grown seedlings indoors, like tomato plants will harden them by putting them outdoors longer and longer on cooler nights above freezing, gradually getting them ready to survive the transplant. I know of the practice of bruising a tomato plant to make it stronger overall. What practices do you use to strengthen your plants?

I've read of some Christians who take cold showers as a spiritual practice. Others see winter as a time for restocking and reforming their faith. What are you doing to build faith and produce fruit? What else will you do to strengthen your faith?

What do you think God has done to strengthen your faith?

Can you be fruitful out of season? Write down your answer why for both yes and no.

Here are some Bible verses that you are invited to change into prayers. They can be for you, your family, church, neighbors, community, or strangers.

Colossians 2:6-7

Psalm 92:12-15

Luke 13:6-9

Matthew 3:8

If you have a young plant in a small container and can do so, put an encouraging verse or quote about growing beside it and place it in the refrigerator for a brief time. As you can move the plant into other areas of the house to be a visual symbol of growing and producing in different places. You can do this "planting" as a prayer reminder or think of God the Creator whenever you see the indoor plant. Why do we need visual reminders to help us grow?

What are some spiritual practices you have to help you produce fruit and evaluate whether you are fruitful in the first place?

Last week I walked into my backyard and saw a tree that is dying. I was surprised because it had survived a storm a few years ago, so I hadn't cut it down. Now I have a decision to make this spring. You can walk about your yard or garden, looking for the plants you have kept that are no longer fruitful or flourishing. What will you do? Do you need to wait and try to reenact the unfruitful tree's parable to try to give it another chance to produce or destroy it now for not being useful?

How does delay or waiting in your gardening show grace? When does it not?

Most fruit trees need other fruit trees to be fruitful. All of them need God. It may help your fruitfulness to collect stories from others about a time they gave or got a second chance. It may also help to have some stories collected that show when letting go of unfruitful things actually was best. Try to put one of each below and compare them to note the differences. End with a prayer based on your insights.

Prayers:

God Plays with Food

As a parent, I wanted my kids to enjoy gardening, so I tried to capture their imagination. We grew purple green beans that changed to green when boiled. We planted bull's-eye beets, blue corn, and yellow watermelon.

The point was to challenge what they thought they knew. I encouraged us all to try new things. I wanted to see what happens, and I still do! This year will feature me growing an almond tree. It was a risk when my zone is border line to what works best, yet it was worth trying to continue to explore God's amazing creation.
When have you tried to grow unusual things or not usually attempted in your area?

What do you know that amazes and excites you about gardens and gardening?

What has surprised you or filled you with wonder?

Please look at these Bible verses to focus on the blessings and joy God reveals to us. What do you see?

Jeremiah 29:5

Isaiah 58:11

Psalm 103:15

Romans 12:2

Genesis 1:12

Create your own words of praise and thanksgiving to offer God here in this space:

If you observe the plants you are starting to grow, do you see any growth? If you don't see any growth, how do you know if it needs anything to grow?

Some of my growing adventures included trying to grow items in containers rather than in the ground. I tried strawberries, corn (in a screened-in porch, too), potatoes in a container, and pole green beans as a houseplant. List or describe any container gardens, unusual garden alternatives (like water or hydroponic gardens), or unique plants that you have tried to grow.

If you could grow anything (no matter the climate), what would you grow that you have not yet tried? Why?

When you start a new ministry or try a new spiritual practice, what are the pros and cons to beginning in a safe space versus launching it fully visible and all out?

How do we determine the size of a container for planting a new plant or ministry? When are these limits that we've self-imposed detrimental? Where can they be best employed?

As we think about growing new things, what do we need to know to challenge us not to make assumptions based on previous experiences?

Who are the plant experts in your life? The spiritual growth experts? The ministry ones? Are there any crossovers in the people or advice?

Looking at the unexpected in gardening in what we grow or where we grow, what are some ways you can think differently about your spiritual development?

After you answer, create a plan to try it out for at least a week and report on it.

Take the time to go online or through a paperback seed catalog. Mark off anything unusual or different that you would be interested in growing or finding out more about and share what they are here to have this for future reference.

Make a video or picture about a garden of wonder. If you want to get more creative, make a container that visualizes or symbolizes a garden of wonder. The reason you are doing this is to have a "prayer garden" image you can focus on to remind you to find wonder and enjoy God's mastering gardening.

What kind of symbol, logo, or conceptualization do you have made for a new ministry that will help people understand and focus on its vision for the glory of God?

Please use this space to journal about your gardening experience at this halfway point through the book.

Perennial Parables

You've seen reenactments of Bible stories, especially during Christmas and Lent. You may have had field trips to learn about sheep or fishing or camping in the "wilderness." If you've gone to the Holy Land or taken other historical faith journeys, you can understand how extra knowledge helps you relate to Biblical times and people. I am asking you to extend this a bit further today.

Look up some of the parables Jesus told and stories about gardening or seeds. Pick one to try out, even if you adapt it slightly. If you want to reenact the parable of the sower, for example, you may want to use untreated seeds collected from your grocery fruit and vegetables or birdseed to allow animals to safely eat what you toss onto a driveway, walk, or gravel area. If you want to sow in the morning and evening like in Ecclesiastes 11, you may want to take a flashlight.

Which parable or practice did you try?

I tried out the parable of the sower. One heirloom seed company offered a variety package of seeds traditionally grown in Haiti. Part of the proceeds would go to help a charity there, which I found inspiring. I got to grow new things like amaranth, mustard, hot peppers, and okra. I thought it would be exciting to eat foods from another country.

To be like the sower, I wanted to give every seed a chance. I didn't have four kinds of ground, but I scattered seeds like the sower, mixing them in the soil with no rows or markers, tossing each kind out on the tilled soil randomly.

I found out that you can't weed if you don't know what you're growing. There are reasons not to plant two kinds of seeds in the same soil. And I found out that sowing seeds without a plan makes it harder to grow and harvest them.

Yet, there were wonders in unexpected discovery. Mustard seeds do grow amazingly, and I have stood beside delicate branches on a stem as tall as me in my backyard. I've harvested amaranth and learned how to eat it. What have you learned from growing new or heirloom seeds?

Take some time to read and make notes about growing from these verses below:

Matthew 13: 1-32

Genesis 2:4-15

Luke 13:18-19

Mark 4:26-29

While the point of a parable may not be to relive it, we can understand its impact by physically doing some similar activity as a memory-making spiritual practice. If we are not avid gardeners, it allows us the chance to grasp what isn't easy to put into words. If we are not comfortable or quick to connect things, this helps us with our analogy thinking and provides context. We can look for ways to appreciate or see them with a new perspective as we pray to grow in God's love through God's Word. What are some ways you have to really get a deeper engagement with scriptures?

I suggest you look to farmers and gardeners for more learning. It's amazing how many resources are out there to help with plants. The book's whole reason was not just to grow a love of plants and creation as I have but to gain the implicit growing understanding that Jesus' first listeners would have known without explanations.

They already knew how hard it is to weed without ruining some precious crop seedlings. They already experienced the heat of the day and the amount of work needed in the vineyard to have the same sense of outrage and confusion of the workers in the vineyard receiving equal pay. They already wondered at the extravagance of the sower in all soils.

We may not have the same context in our gardens – some with irrigation systems and some with water hoses or mine with a plastic pitcher I also use to drink from myself. Still, we get that plants need water and appreciate living water that we would never have to work again to get.

Use this day to send emails or make calls. I do it all the time when I am curious or trying to connect with others. Find out some answers to questions or ask for advice.

List five questions you have about plants, gardens, growing:

1.

2.

3.

4.

5.

Go back and list where you can look for answers and the date you did so. Finally, when you do find an answer or at least another person that you've been referred to next, list that as well. You may not get responses, and that is part of growing. You keep going and find out where you can.

It would be easy to say that you should do the same for a ministry. List questions, where to find answers, and the effort you made. But we wouldn't reenact the parable of the Sower in this way.

People generally don't appreciate unsolicited advice or help. That is why, even as well-meaning as we can be, the special book we give someone, the article we send as a link to let someone know we were thinking of them can be unappreciated or unused. We sow seeds that bear no fruit, especially if we are prescriptive and trying to solve someone else's problem that we think we have perceived.

The parable is about giving good news, not things. We aren't looking for gratitude or acknowledgment either. So we could continue, or we could try to choose other things like encouraging cards to show we care.

But here's the thing I would like you to consider. Giving in the four fields. Whether good news or encouragement, whatever you sow, can you sow in the fields that are paved, rocky, or thorn invested? Think about what that means in ministry.

If you live where there is little chance it will be useful or quickly forgotten or cut down by others or distractions, is this something God will say, "well done, my good and faithful servant?"

I think it is easy to reenact the parable with just seeds or even seed money, but are you willing to go into those fields to work? In the path or paved kind of soil, you'll have to shelter from predators and conditions that increase vulnerability and being out in the open. I mean the main question is whether the sower stays to do this because we know that it could be the job of the workers tending the seeds that are to grow. You'll have initial success in the rocky soil but then fight against conditions that don't favor sustainability. In the thorns and weeds, you'll have some success but constantly compete for resources and attention to keep going.

In giving the good news, we have seeds that are sown, but we need workers that keep working with God to grow that good news within someone. We see a gardener extravagant in spreading the good news everywhere, knowing the results. Still, we also need to be the extravagant workers continuing to feed and develop the good news with God's help to still give the chance to everyplace the good news is given.

Where is your paved road impossible to grow place for ministry? How do you pray for it?

Where is your rocky soil, good start but quickly dying place for ministry? Is it in the church or outside?

Where is your thorny, struggling to survive against the weeds, place for ministry? How do you get into it without getting entangled or distracted?

Where is your appreciative, growing good soil place of ministry? How does it help the others?

How do we get over the need for validation or results? We want to be good stewards, we tell ourselves, but we also know that we want some joy in seeing growth and feeling part of it. We sometimes need to share some of the muddiness from our minds. Try this to start. List five things you have no interest in/do not like.

1.

2.

3.

4.

5.

Now circle the things above that God has an interest in or does like. If you shared reptiles or green peppers as I did in doing this activity, you might admit that if God created these things, he might be interested in them. He might also like that nosy neighbor or the screech of crows even if he doesn't like other things we could list like sin or unhappiness.

In prayer walk the talk activities, I ask people to think about how they love others enough to take an interest in someone else's passion. They will learn about dinosaurs or fly fishing for the sake of a child or spouse. They will help and encourage a golfer or knitter even if they cannot find that interest in themselves. Part of sowing and letting God care for the results in us and others is to pray for God's will and what God is interested in. So, below, would you write a prayer to God for the things you do not like and have no interest in?

In this way, we understand a love that reaches out to what we consider impossibly unlovable or unchangeable. When we get to the parable and doing it, like this gardening, we are developing the empathy and growth mindset of God's kingdom. That we sometimes choose to love where and who makes no sense because there is no reciprocation.

There are so many gardens we'll never see the results. The tree planted in a forest far away in memory of someone else's loved one. The plants that a camp grew from your ideas in a location half a country away. The seed program offering unused seeds to schools or community gardens. The charity that teaches people half a world away how to start a business and profit from growing different crops. And there are those that never sprout and grow.

Once I asked a wealthy church to use some extra funds to give to a struggling church as seed money. I suggested that it could be anonymous, with no strings attached. It wouldn't have to be that much, even a token gift, to let that smaller church know that others in the community believed in its ministries and that it would grow again. It didn't happen, the money went for their own ministries. Years have passed and whether coincidence or results, the churches have almost reversed roles.

Do I think the broadcast method is something to do without thought or direction, or hope? No, not any more than I think you randomly cast a line for fishing. You do try to do your best work even if you broadcast in unlikely places.

What does it mean to support a ministry or start one that may not last or be sustainable? It may be that small growth that is at the right time and place for the right person. It might also be the catalyst to encourage other risk-taking sowers.

In the online course I teach using this book, the day's topic is called Perennial Parables so I kept the title here. Do you understand the irony? We have to be willing to plant perennially and grow annually. The parable doesn't change. We do each time we plant persistently and proactively.

For the wrap-up of this chapter, can you list the perennial and annual ministries you serve?

What is the difference in why and how you care for these?

What would happen if you gave your sowing in a different field? Would you ever teach a class in a church that is not your own? Would you help a nonprofit that is not a passion of yours?

If so, what would be the way to ensure their success? What would you have to do and NOT do?

Paul Planted and Apollos Watered

My daughter was asked to water and care for a neighbor's extensive garden. The neighbor hid little notes around the planters for her to find as proof she had done the task each time. My daughter said, "Mom, she made watering harder than it needed to be." I thought this extra micromanaging was just because she was a teenager but I learned age doesn't matter.

When I started working at one church, I had two different leaders tell me how to water the three plants in the office. One stressed that I water only from the top and the other emphasized watering only from the bottom with a sign on the plant to remind me. There was no way to please both of them so I watered sparingly, half on top and half at the bottom. Sometimes I alternated the method I was ordered to do for all of the plants. My solutions must have upset one of the church members because two plants were moved to the restroom. The other person had left her spider plant in the office. I thought, at least I was trusted to water this plant. A year later, I found out that she was coming to the church on Saturdays to water her plant, not trusting I would do so during the week.

What are your stories about caring for others' plants or asking others to care for yours?

Your assignment is now to be on the other side. Invite someone to do some form of care for the plants you have. This can be all or some of them and involve any kind of care. If you are indoors and don't have an outdoor garden, you could ask someone to take a plant and "plant sit" for a few days. Come back later to fill in what happened and how you felt.

Read aloud 1 Corinthians 3:1-9 and pray about whatever comes to mind from this.

Start by reading and taking notes from 2 Corinthians 9:6 and 1 Corinthians 3:1-9

Pray for the people you've asked to help with your garden and the people you've asked for help with your questions.
How did your gardening collaboration go?

Did you give instructions or allow the other person to figure out the task? Why?

Compare the asking for temporary help with how you hand over a ministry. For example, this could be someone substituting to teach your class versus giving control of that class to them permanently. What's the difference in approach, if any?

In what ways does your church facilitate a transition in leadership?

Is there training, or is the new person allowed and encouraged to do it their own way?

Find Bible verses that share how leaders collaborate, equip, or let their leadership go to another. These can be positive or negative examples and advice. Tell which passages you chose. How might they relate them to gardening and growing? What do plants teach us about these topics?

How would a community garden help teach leadership and collaboration? What other lessons would be useful for you, your family, or your church?

What stories do you want to share about working with others or stepping back from leadership that have now come to mind?

I've had some interesting ministry transitions. I planned all the spiritual development programs, the curriculum, and activities to help develop faith in one job. As part of my work, I began teaching them how to assess what they were learning and preferred in their small group context. In the next five years, we went from an adult ministry completely controlled and determined by the director to one in which each group took leadership and ownership of their own process. They learned to see their patterns and needs. They also collaborated with others, such as the children and youth ministries and some of the intergenerational and family activities. The leaders of each small group found the resources and planned their learning and outreach. It was a blessing that the adult ministries program, with all its small groups, was able to "run itself" after I left for more than six months until my position was filled by combining it with the associate pastor's role.

I tried to develop leadership on a smaller scale too. Once I took a Sunday school class about following great leaders and how we step into someone else's shoes and decide what/how to make our own. Halfway through this lesson, I surprised that class by asking them if they wanted to take over the teaching. It was an interesting moment, but it fit the class and discussion we had been having. And, wonders of wonders, they did it! They facilitated a class on leadership and included me as a peer in the continued discussion. So how do you develop leaders?

What are your beliefs about leadership? For example, should a leader start slow and adapt to the context, or should they come in and make it their own immediately?

Are there any exceptions to the rules of leadership you have?

When you think of your leading ministries and calls by God, which ones come to mind?

Why do you need to have mentors as a leader? Why do you need to be a mentor when you lead?

I think leaders might see themselves as gardeners. But I worry that this makes it seem like the other people are not seen as equal. They could be assumed to be the workers or even the plants! How do leaders stay servants and keep humble?

It may be easier to be compared to being plants together under God's gardening? How would you describe your garden's growth in your ministry – and what season are you in?

What are some ways as a leader you can facilitate your ministry's growth (garden) as a whole?

What might you do for one or two in your ministry to help the whole overall?

I have read and seen so many things that are supposed to help only tomatoes or only roses. I've also seen the general enrichment materials that are guaranteed to make the entire garden grow. If you could only choose, would you concentrate on something for the whole garden, or would you want to focus on a specific crop or flower to improve?

How do you make these same kinds of decisions in leadership of what to focus on?

Make an action plan. List two things you will do from this leadership chapter to help your garden and help your ministry grow. Be sure to include a deadline to finish these steps.

Finding A Place to Grow

While I have been interested in growing heirloom and unique seeds, I also support native Pennsylvanian plants and avoid invasive species that are aggressive growers or damaging to local plants. Although I love to consider the bamboo in my reflections on how faith can grow, for example, I don't want to grow it myself.

I still enjoy walks in the woods where I can see the jewelweed, May apples, and mountain laurel. It pleases me to find teaberries and wild blueberries, know the difference between club moss and crow's feet, and seek trailing arbutus and bluetts.

Because of this, various parsonages had wildflowers included in my gardening. I tried to grow a Jack-in-the-Pulpit always (obviously), but others like trillium are also favorites to try now. I appreciate the subtler beauty of some plants like shy lady's slippers over the domesticated orchids. One of the strangest and most impressionable lessons I had as a third-grade child was our teacher stopping class and marching all out to the adjacent woods to see a rare lady's slipper. I couldn't get over that the teacher would change our schedule just to see a wildflower. I never forgot the wonder in this.

We have a responsibility to be stewards of God's creation. It is interesting for you to decide if this means all the plants or just the domesticated ones. So I ask: Do you garden with the plants that you want to preserve for the future or focus on those plants you can use yourself today?

Go ahead and read these scriptures. The notes here can also be tied into what you think others might see in the verses so that you read looking for more than one idea or perspective. Summarize what they are saying to the church or our personal spiritual development. Important to add: What are they not saying to us?

I often ask to find out what sticks out for you, but I'd also ask that you look for the smaller things that you don't think others notice or that you haven't before. This can be like seeing the native plants, the smaller wildflowers versus those we are familiar with and commonly grow/see.

Luke 12:27-28, 1 Peter 1:23-24

Psalm 104:14, Isaiah 61:11

Isaiah 35:1-2, Deuteronomy 8:17

What are your native plants around you? How did you learn about them? Who taught you?

Invasive species are a bit more problematic. Do we count mint or lamb's ears that will not be controlled in the yard? What are your "invasive" species?

How should we classify and feel about kudzu used along highways for ground cover or the bamboo and palms some people nearby have tried to grow?

Skim Romans 3 and read about why Paul wrote the letter to the Romans. What do we do about divided churches and us versus them groupings of people?

Pray Psalm 130

One of the problems with analogy thinking is that you can become so good that you start to make connections beyond what may be intended or useful. Sometimes it is good NOT to compare or judge. This whole book, I have been asking you to make connections with different ideas, and yet we need to be careful that our own thinking doesn't become "invasive" and take over with ideas or analogies that don't belong.

Where do you see people taking analogies and generalizations too far? In what ways can we prevent this or challenge our assumptions about our beliefs or biases?

How do we define what belongs and what doesn't to a particular place? Who determines what causes a negative impact on the surroundings or others?

Think about the future. Which of the native/invasive species on the list you made will stay the same and which may change categories someday? Why?

What responsibilities do we have for our planting choices now?

What legacy do we leave in our gardening and growing decisions? Does this tie into the church, or should we not make the connection to how things work in nature?

If you could help grow any particular wild plant or create favorable conditions for its sustainability, what plant would it be and why?

If you could help any organization outside the church or create connections that would help it for the future, what would it be and why did you choose it?

One of the struggles we have is whether we see ourselves of this world or not. We have the hope in Jesus' return, but we are to be working until then in our earthly garden. We have to be careful not to label people as native or invasive, as insiders or outsiders. I believe we need to foster ministries with others and not for others in most cases. What are the struggles you see in working for God right here on earth?

It can be easy to plant a garden. It can be easy to give a donation, feed a person, or visit them once. Perhaps the appeal of wildflowers is that we don't have to care for them. When we plant a garden, are we committing to seeing it through to harvest or looking at handing it off?

When we help feed or visit someone once, are we called to take the next step and even learn their name? What are other next steps that tend the people as the ministry?

I hope it has helped you to find out about your native plants. To know where they are, their names, and perhaps even some history. Whether you decide to connect this to ministry, the practice of loving God's creation is implied. I remember my mother taking me deep into the woods to a honeysuckle tree. She was so overjoyed to have found it, and the problem was that as a kid trying to look on my own, I couldn't do it. Only when it was in bloom, with that distinct smell, could I find it.

I don't know how many of you have had a childhood like mine. I was taken to "strippings," unreclaimed coal mined land with lots of shale and plants just starting to come back. There were findings of wild strawberries, grapes, and elderberries. There were fossil hunts that only found ferns. In the meadows beside my home, I used to name all the flowers until it was fenced in for cattle and horses. I was allowed (until I was a teenager) to roam the woods even past a boney pile (an underground coal mine entrance). Both woods that I called my second home had a stream to cross.

Ironically, being a girl, it was no longer safe for me to be in my beloved woods and wilderness alone once a few homeless men had used our woods for camping out. To this day, I envy those who can so easily go alone into the wild places because that fear of what was once my sanctuary still lingers. Even now, it is hard to trust and go where I once did as such a dreamy and wonder-filled child.

Have you ever had a fear of the wilderness put into you? If so, how did you recapture that love of your youth? If you haven't, how would you help someone not to fear but appreciate this different kind of garden?

I've tried to overcome the dread of the woods that I still love deeply. I've applied and gotten several interviews to run camps and whole camping programs. I even made it to the second round on the biggest one I tried to get as my ministry. I've supported the wilderness and woods and even gone on those walks by myself.

You see, I am sharing here so that you will get to your fears. We can try to garden the wilderness or visit it, but it is not tamed, and it does contain its dangers and evils. What is the wilderness (literally or figuratively) that you most fear and why?

What have you done to overcome your fear? Has God asked you to go there? What do you pray?

It may connect to your greatest ministry fear. It may not here. But what is your call and where?

Hope: Buried Treasure

My friend Rhoda is in charge of the greenhouses at Cornell. She is responsible for providing education on biodiversity and the cultivation of rare plants. But I write because she does something else. She connects her passion for gardening with empathy and healing. During one of the recent awful events in our nation (does it matter which one as much as how many it could be?), she gave students bulbs to plant.

Yet first, she had them write down their hopes and dreams on these tiny slips of paper. She asked the students to bury the slips of paper with their bulbs and keep coming back over the spring to see the plants' progress, a tangible reminder of life persisting and blooming despite the loss.

It made me wonder if the students did some cultivating of these hopes and dreams in other ways as the plants grew. Still, all I know from her is how meaningful the planting event was and how much the students appreciated being able to do something in that tragic time. They did keep coming back too.

What hopes and dreams and growing do you see here?

Jeremiah 17:7-8, Genesis 1:11

Hebrews 6:7, Psalm 126:6.

James 5:7, Galatians 6:9

[Jesus said] *"The kingdom of heaven is like treasure hidden in a field. When a man found it, he hid it again, and then in his joy went and sold all he had and bought that field."* Matthew 13:44

Did you notice? The field the man was looking in wasn't his. He was honorable in that he didn't take the treasure but bought the field. Yet this leads to so many other questions. If the treasure was hidden, how did he find it? Why was he in the field? Was he working in it as a hired hand? Was he leasing it to farm? Was he digging or planting to find the hidden treasure in the field? What do you think?

Look around you for the unused, underused, and abandoned fields. What are other churches and community spots doing with their land and surroundings?

Can't go out? Are there hidden possibilities indoors for growing faith gardens?

We are not to mistake the field for the treasure or the garden. Jesus gives an analogy about the great value of the Kingdom of Heaven and the response to finding it. Yet I think we can help point people to heaven by digging for it, even seeing our work as treasure hunters.

Write an update on the seeds you have planted as a gardening journal record. It is good to be aware of the stories we are in the midst of making as well as the ones from our past!

Share what other churches, neighbors, or friends are doing with their cultivations. Are there any ways to partner and learn from them? How do you see gardening as a way to connect with others in new ways?

What is the Kingdom of God like? Bring in some other Bible passages or paint us a picture of words. What does it look like as an individual or as a church to sell all for it?

Do you have any treasure hunt stories to offer? If you want this to relate to gardening, ever found something extra or exciting such as at a harvest?

Gift your future self with a prayer as a treasure to share today.

Sometimes I imagine what we could do with that hope that we have buried and want to grow again. Are there some hopes from your past that you wish to ask God to rejuvenate?

Sometimes we can help others with their hopes. Do you remember the story of "The Secret Garden" and how the girl had asked for a bit of land of her very own? Did you ever have those longings too?

Perhaps you can lend land personally or as a church to someone to grow what they want, even providing them with "seed money." I know one church that had a space given to those with mental illnesses, and they would gather by their tiny vegetable garden in fellowship. Some even joined our Bibles studies. Another church in Wisconsin taught gardening to those with special needs or disabilities, using a raised garden to grow something of their own. Who are the people you could reach and share in growing together?

Read Psalm 24:1, Matthew 5:5, Exodus 23:10-11, Hebrews 13:16, John 4:35, Ruth 2:15. What do you see in these verses?

How can you give someone such as a child, a neighbor, or a family member a chance to grow something they want to grow and help them if they want this? (Perhaps we can grow plants in such a way that we "think" them by giving our extra seedlings/seeds away.)

We may not be in a situation where we can provide space for others, especially if our gardening is in containers or indoors. While you might give out an extra container, I'd like you to think of other possibilities too. Some churches I know sell house plants at their fundraising yard sales and bazaars. I am always surprised to find out these are usually some of the first items that sell out. We have faithful gardeners of these plants who enlist others to grow them too. Maybe it's the nice containers or the kind of plants that are grown. I don't know. But it is community gardening in a sense, even if the plants are not at the same location.

What makes a good and successful community garden? Is there a difference between "good" and "successful"?

How might you connect with an inner-city or landlocked downtown church to do community gardening?

What other ministries might grow from sharing your land or resources with others?

Why do you think there are conflicts over others' yards or gardens? What are the root causes of not being able to maintain a community garden?

How can you show appreciation to gardening experts for what they provide or teach?

Research gardening or produce competitions and share more about the winners. How are they chosen? What are the criteria?

I asked you to look into what others see as successful gardens and crops. If you've done any research on community gardens, you'll note some kinds are communal to work together and kinds that lease the land for each person to plant as their own. In some ways, we do this in churches too.

We offer to collaborate and work together toward a common "crop" or ministry goal, and then there are the kinds of ministries that are territorial with fences and silos. Each person has their area to produce ministry goals like worship, music, children's programs, and the expertise is emphasized over the labor time and effort. We become good at one crop.

The problems with communal gardens can be the lack of leadership and organization, while the problems with each person taking a section of the community garden for their own can be the lack of collaboration and communication. What are your experiences here?

Take a few minutes to think of the gardening ideas you have been gathering and trying out. How would you get others to join in gardening if they were not good at it or had never tried?

How would you get experts in gardening and growing plants to allow others to join in?

Which are you—the newbie or the church expert? How can you nurture the other that you aren't?

Biblical Garden Adventure

My year of growing Biblical plants was also an adventure. I wanted to grow the foods mentioned in the Bible which led to a fascinating search of what I could grow that year to eat versus what wouldn't work due to the time or climate involved.

It reminded me of a pastor in Texas, Jason Valendy, who said that he wished God gave "vegetables of the Spirit" because they grow quickly compared to fruit. I totally relate to this. I am not always patient! Why did God ask us to grow fruit instead?

I chose cucumbers, melons, and then one long-term commitment, figs for my garden that year. I found varieties grown in countries closer to Biblical countries than American varieties to be more accurate. I had a secret weapon, an aged organic pesticide using red pepper flakes. Turns out rabbits have exotic tastes, too and appreciated the salad dressing. I lost my garden and fig trees. I've learned not to underestimate the tenacity of the predators of my garden, even those that seem the most harmless of all. It was the garden without harvest that year. What gardens have you had that were like this? .

Read these verses: Numbers 11:5, Mark 11:12-14, Jeremiah 24:1-10, and Song of Solomon 2:15and comment on them together as a whole. What notes, observations or insights do you want to keep?

Do some gardening if you can today that deters the garden competition (like weeding, measures that prevent insects, or actions that drive away animals), and that enhances or helps the garden's collaborators (bring in some garden helpers like marigolds or worms) or plant bee-friendly flowers in a safe space for them to gather. What did you do today to help your gardening and to care for plants?

Did you focus on the prevention/protection side of the gardening or the encouragement of collaborators/growth side?

What are the implications and connections in ministry?

Compare the garden and church. What do you see? Now whatever your answer is, compare it to your life and being.

There is something about growing plants to connect with your heritage, whether it is your faith family tree or your biological one. When I asked for advice about this course from Clare Hescox, a certified master gardener, she said, "Don't forget about the slips of plants that people take from a family member to grow on their own." She referred to the cuttings people do of rose bushes or trees that they want to try to preserve for either the plant's sake or the memory of that loved one or location. What are your experiences with cuttings or slips from plants?

It reminded me that the oak trees at my kids' high school. Each graduating senior would touch the oak trees before getting their diploma on graduation day, a tradition that went back many decades to connect them to all the other graduates in past years.

Those trees were grown from slips of the original oaks that had been part of the old high school. We were told that slips were being grown from those trees to ensure that the tradition could continue no matter how long the current trees lived.

If you can get a cutting from a plant you'd like to grow either for sentimental reasons or to replace a plant in the future, please do so. Watch a video on "propagating a slip" to help you.
What did you choose to try to grow?

Note: If you cannot do this cutting, please use something from your refrigerator like a root vegetable top cut off and put in a lid with water or cutting out and placing a potato peel with the eyes in a dish of water in the sunlight.

Read these Bible verses: Job 14:7, Isaiah 11:1, Psalm 80:8, Ezekiel 17:22-23 and make any notes you'd like to have here.

Pray about the transplants and second chance growth opportunities God gives. Where are you praying this in your life? Where in the church and beyond into the community?

What will you do if it doesn't take root?

Pray about John 15:4-11. Where and when do you see churches or people trying to branch out on their own? What can we do about it? How do we ask others to keep us rooted and abiding in Christ?

Do you have any other second chance gardening stories to share, such as a plant that came back or what you grew from a scrap or slip?

What are the ministries or dormant things in your church that you could try to transplant or re-grow? What would you need for this to have the best chance to succeed?

When is there a time to let go of a particular plant or ministry, and how do you know?

Gardens can grow over long stretches of time, just as one man took forty years to grow a forest by planting trees each day. It reminds me that God is very patient as he lets us work to build His kingdom through our growing and tending our gardens of faith. We have to look for the everlasting growth he is providing. When we abide in him we're more excited to share what God is doing for us than what we are doing for him.

If you walk around a place that you have lived or a family member has, what are the plants and gardens that have been there the longest? What are your memories that you can slip into this book to keep and think about as you grow from here?

What are some memories of gardens that others have shared with you? How do they help you in your growing?

Use this space to make a list of what you want to share and keep the stories going. Remember that you can use social media, calls, artwork, or even signs in the garden itself to make meaning and connect with God.

Why stop at only creating Biblical or prayer gardens? There can be musical gardens (with chimes or plants with music names/looks), praise gardens, power gardens, compassion gardens, mystery gardens, sensory gardens, and so on. Use your imagination and share some ideas here.

One time I bought bulbs that were supposedly "Cartwright crocus" that bloomed in the fall instead of the spring. While I was undoubtedly swindled and planted flowers that never grew, my imagination was stirred about the possibilities of what else might be out there to try and grow! What can you find to grow?

Are there plants with your name or somehow connected to a place or item important to you?

As this chapter explored the heritage plants we can grow for various reasons, it helps us think of our churches' heritage in us. Just as the Hebrews longed for a return to Egypt because of the food, we can cling to our heritage in the same way. Think of the church(es) you've belonged to over the years. What are the items or traditions that resonate or stay with you?

What happens when we try to transplant or grow these in other places?

Why might it be good to do this connecting to our past? When does our heritage stunt our growth in faith?

Wheat Fields

Once when I wanted my kids to learn about wheat, I asked someone from church to help me get some to show them. The friend asked a farmer who sent along a bunch for Sunday school, and it got even better from there.

I researched and found a place that did demonstrations of milling wheat like the pioneers, a hands-on workshop that I asked Hanover Street Elementary to offer to all the kids. Students in the school got to grind seeds to make flour by hand and learn other farming processes and working in pioneer days.

I took my kids to a historical mill in Maryland (Union Mills) and bought them flour to try out in our cooking. We even learned some Civil War history that was a part of the reason the mill still exists. The war that divided families helped preserve unexpected legacies in other ways. I was trying to bond with my family here.

I next learned about making bread as they did in Biblical times and then making the clay oven and then making the clay. Always learning, always like a kid looking for more!

The point is that I took gardening to another level by learning from others and expanding the topic to new fields.

To look into this further, read and reflect on these verses:

John 12:24, Psalm 81:6

Ruth 2, Luke 10:2

Proverbs 10:5, Genesis 8:2

Leviticus 23:22

Now let's talk harvest. Why on earth am I doing this? Do you remember the Bible verse that tells us, *"Jesus replied, "No one who puts a hand to the plow and looks back is fit for service in the kingdom of God." (Luke 9:62)* It seems I shouldn't ask you to look back at all!

I have my reasons! I only want to give a quick look back to prepare to move forward. We are not dwelling there; we are pausing to harvest our learning and faith. If that doesn't work for you, think of this as if this were the winter or fallow season before we grow again. What are your harvest stories and encouragements?

What do you talk about when you are working with others in the field? Have you ever gone berry or fruit picking at a farm to find out? Are there any harvests (even of flowers) that you can do now?

Look today at how you can garden-- using information! You can plant ideas like seeds; you can experience lessons on growing and letting path lead to path in your spiritual journey.

You could do this same sort of study on animals and how we care for them, even providing experiences fishing or helping at a farm.

You could make this same sort of connection and spiritual growth practices with camping and forming clay pots and cooking and running races and sailing and building things.

You could offer this kind of experiential and discussion format as a look at prayers and prayer walks, developing the conversation around the hands-on things we do. You could do even more gardening and growing. Pray about this and where God is leading you next. What ideas and calls do you see now?

Take stock of the various plants you have been growing while journaling in this book. Pray about their progress and yours. How do you *"Taste and see that the Lord is good?"*

What are the next steps you will do from this?

Do you remember how the book started with the empty rows to fill with your writing? These words were like the seeds you planted. Of course, you need to end the same way. But, before you write your reflections and questions, pray.

By now I hope you can see gardens everywhere, in lines of music, in the roads and forests, even in the buildings and cities. You can write whatever you want, lyrics, poetry, praise, prose. I recommend prayers and scriptures, but just grow your field and finish well.

The harvest is ready, and you, the worker, are due to gather in the fruit and grow the seeds of faith into trees that produce, protect, and offer a place for others to grow too. Be free writing!

Bibliography

1. The writing process. (n.d.). Retrieved March 24, 2021, from https://writingprocess.mit.edu/process/step-1-generate-ideas/instructions/freewriting
2. Genesis 3:6
3. 1 Kings 21
4. Matthew 21:33-44
5. Genesis 4:2-8
6. Genesis 3:17-19
7. Lexter. (n.d.). Comparing French vs English Garden Landscaping. Retrieved March 24, 2021, from https://insights.jonite.com/comparing-french-vs-english-garden-landscaping
8. John 9:1-12
9. Cottage garden. (2021, March 02). Retrieved March 24, 2021, from https://en.wikipedia.org/wiki/Cottage_garden
10. Jeremiah 38
11. Psalm 46:10
12. Collison, R. (2020). *Preparing Fields for Seasons of Change*. Trilogy Christian Publishing.
13. Bench grafting with Xander rose At RAINTREE Nursery! (2021, February 19). Retrieved March 24, 2021, from https://youtu.be/Rn0n6aLm8Ow
14. Multiple-Budded fruit Trees: Dave Wilson Nursery. (n.d.). Retrieved March 24, 2021, from https://www.davewilson.com/product-information/category/about-multi-bud-fruit-trees
15. Mark 8:24
16. John 20:11-18
17. Susan Baroncini. Retrieved March 24, 2021, from https://susanbaroncini-moe.com/please-stop-misinterpreting-the-road-not-taken/
18. How to grow a lemon tree from a seed (0-6 months updates). (2020, January 16). Retrieved March 24, 2021, from https://youtu.be/XC67v3q-m28
19. Luke 13:6-9

20. Home. (n.d.). Retrieved March 24, 2021, from https://www.wilsonbrosgardens.com/what-are-chill-hours-for-fruit-plants-trees.html
21. Matthew 13
22. Matthew 20:1-16
23. McCarthy, J. (2017, December 26). A lifetime of planting trees on a Remote River Island: Meet India's Forest man. Retrieved March 24, 2021, from https://www.npr.org/sections/parallels/2017/12/26/572421590/hed-take-his-own-life-before-killing-a-tree-meet-india-s-forest-man
24. Psalm 34:8

About the Author(s)

I want to share how I was greatly influenced by others who love nature and stories. In the tradition of the storyteller Donald Davis, I wanted to find ways to preserve stories of my family and life as a legacy, though this consists of faith as a garden to explore and grow. What you can know about me, you'll find in the book here or look it up somewhere online.

I am an appreciative gardener, not an expert. I wanted you to work on this book as a collaborative effort between us. We will grow a book together, one in which our faith stories intertwine like branches or abiding vines. I've given you some supportive structures to act like a trellis and some tools to promote new growth. I've offered seeds of ideas to germinate and develop. I've turned over the soil and prayed. In a sense, we have be co-authors once you've written in here. I've merely given you room to share your part. Why not include your bio here so that we can share the credit and collectively give the glory to God?

_____

_____

_____

_____

_____

_____

_____

_____

_____

_____

_____

_____

Made in the USA
Coppell, TX
01 September 2022

82481920R00056